Close to Home
Exposed

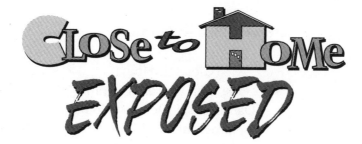

Other Close to Home Collections

Close to Home
One Step Closer to Home
Dangerously Close to Home
Home: The Final Frontier
The Honeymoon Is Over
The Silence of the Lamberts
Striking Close to Home
The Close to Home Survival Guide
Close to Home Uncut
The Scourge of the Vinyl Car Seats
The Get Well Book

Treasuries
Close to Home Revisited
Close to Home Unplugged

Little Books
Give Mommy the Superglue and Other Tips on Surviving Parenthood
What? Another Birthday?!

Also from John McPherson
High School Isn't Pretty
The Barber of Bingo

Close to Home EXPOSED

A Close to Home Collection

JOHN McPHERSON

Andrews McMeel
Publishing

Kansas City

02 03 04 05 06 BAH 10 9 8 7 6 5 4 3 2

ISBN: 0-7407-2672-2

Library of Congress Control Number: 2002102580

Close to Home may be viewed on the Internet at:
www.ucomics.com

Visit the **Close to Home** Web store at:
www.closetohome.com

E-Mail John McPherson at:
closetohome@compuserve.com

To Peter and Griffin

Physics students at Waterburg High School attempt to measure the energy of a sneeze.

"Whoa! Whoa! Dr. Goldfarb, please *slow down*. You're getting way ahead of the insurance paperwork."

"Trust me on this. If we want the dog to bond with the baby right away, he needs to eat all of his meals off your stomach during the third trimester."

At the Slinky Quality Control Center.

"Stan! Wake up! I think I heard a noise!"

"Well, let's see. I can put you in seat 7-A and your kids in 28-C, D and E. Is that far enough apart?"

"...and when every speck of food is gone, the plate will rise, causing the other plate to drop, thereby raising the candle, which will burn through the string and release the chocolate cake."

"Well, that's a good start. But if you *really* want to build a fort, you're going to need a *lot more* logs than that!"

"Mind? Are you kidding? Dad's gonna *love* being able to get the mail while he's still in his underwear!"

Advanced parenting techniques

"Hey, Dawn, watch this! I short-sheeted his bed!"

12

"Well, this whole *el niño* thing sure turned out to be a crock! So it's three degrees warmer than usual. Big deal!"

Thoroughly burned-out by shuttling her kids to and from school activities, Shelley makes a drastic move.

"*Another* 'Fantastic'?! Danny, you have *really* turned your grades around! I am so proud of you!"

"...and when he discovered that his new $2,700 pool table wouldn't fit down the basement stairs, his screaming caused dogs over a half mile away to start howling."

"For the hundredth time, *no*, I don't have the keys to the back of the truck! They're locked in the cab with the others!"

"For an additional $150, would you like our one-year stain-removal service plan?"

"As part of our commitment to employee morale, anyone who isn't near a window is given this scale model of the downtown skyline and three pigeons."

"OK. There are no monsters under your bed!
There will never be monsters under your bed
again, ever! Now get to sleep."

Suddenly, Dave realized the plus side of getting
the last valentine card on the rack.

"All I know is they met on the Internet, and after they each type 'I do,' they'll step forward and meet for the first time."

"Swerved...to...avoid...black...cat."

Mary quickly regretted giving Phil the subscription to Popular Mechanics.

At the Hair Center for Men research laboratory.

"Simple. I pay them a $50-a-month protection fee."

Right from the start, friends and relatives sensed the tension in Jeff and Lisa's marriage.

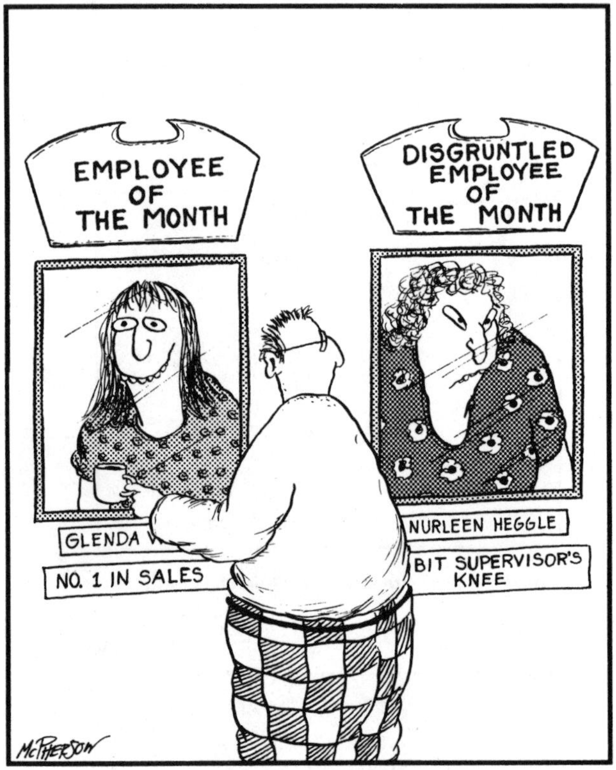
EMPLOYEE OF THE MONTH
DISGRUNTLED EMPLOYEE OF THE MONTH
GLENDA V
NO. 1 IN SALES
NURLEEN HEGGLE
BIT SUPERVISOR'S KNEE
McPHERSON

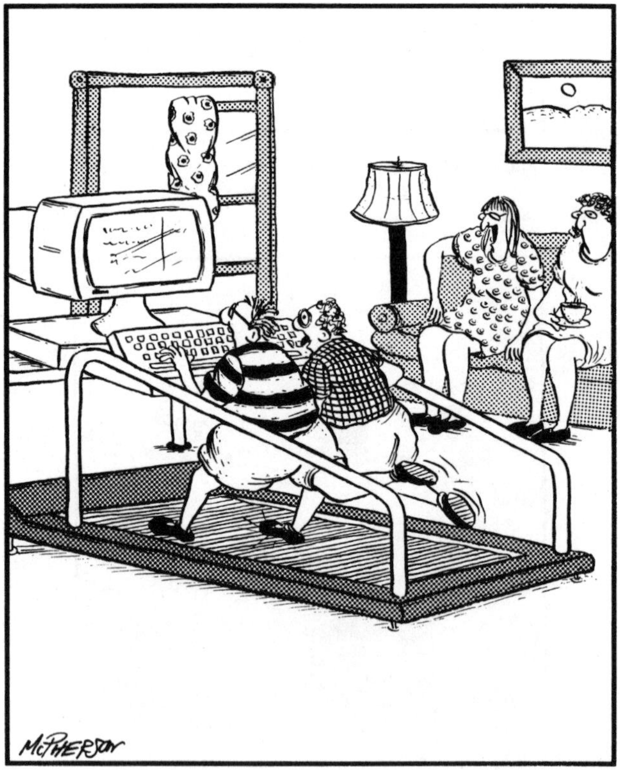
McPHERSON

"Yep, that's the new rule. If they're going to spend all their free time surfing the Net, the treadmill's got to be on."

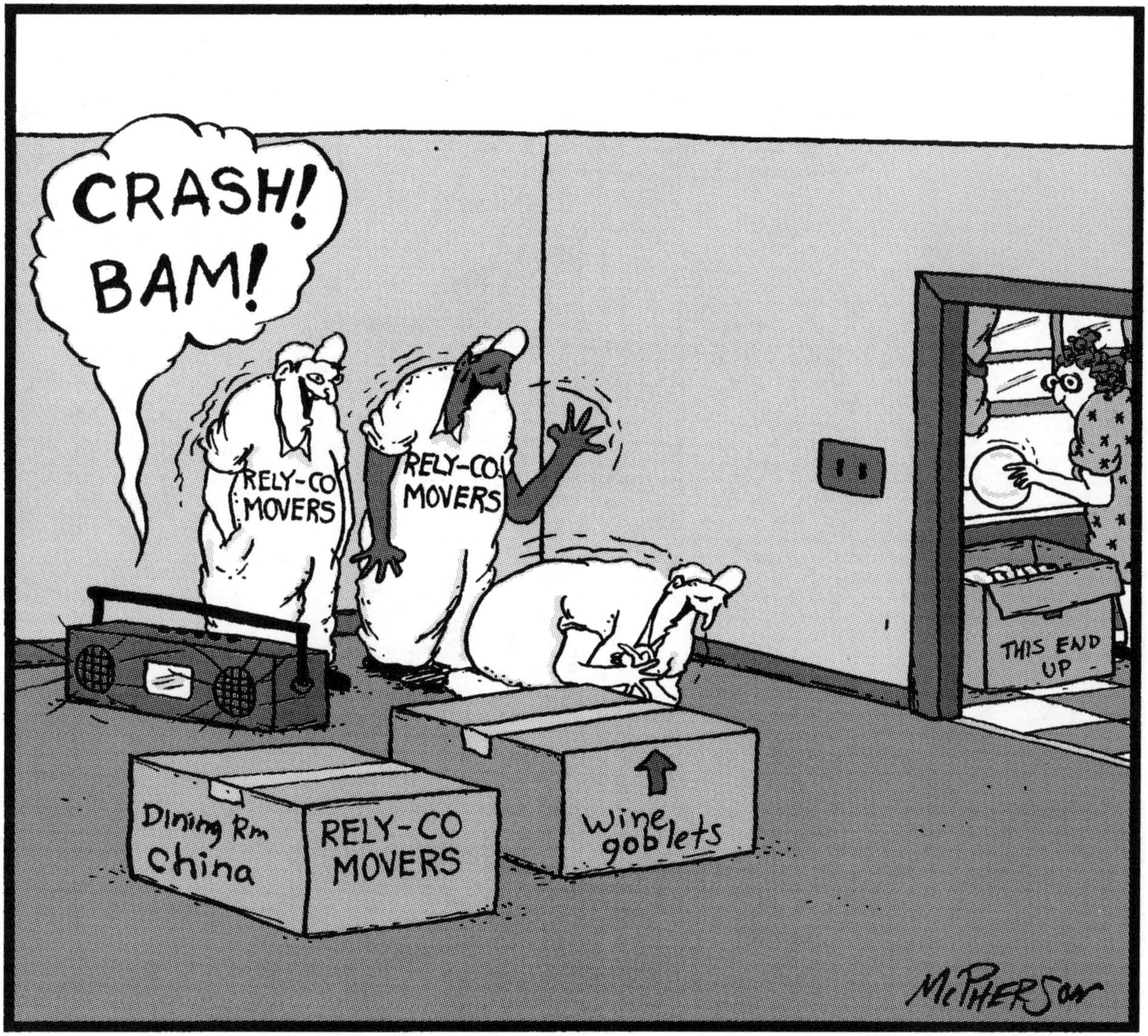
CRASH! BAM!
RELY-CO MOVERS
RELY-CO MOVERS
THIS END UP
Dining Rm china
RELY-CO MOVERS
Wine goblets
McPHERSON

"Calm down, calm down. I found your lucky rabbit's foot in the staff lounge, and Denise will be here with your lucky scalpel in just a minute."

The downside of working for Parker Brothers.

"With this type of artificial heart you may want to consider getting a convertible."

"Aw, come on, Mom. We worked on it all afternoon."

"Head down the right side about 150 yards. If my drive slices, just deflect it back onto the fairway toward the green."

"If you're interested in our premium-rate homeowner's insurance, you simply need to demonstrate that you can fend off prowlers for a minimum of 10 minutes."

"For heaven's sake, if he asks if we want to see the wine list, tell him 'no'!"

"Relax! This is just until the tax assessor comes here tomorrow."

As expected, the new fountain of coffee
did wonders for morale in the office.

"They're all done shoveling the driveway, but they
said their friend Kenny had an unfortunate incident
involving a plow truck."

"In the 42 years we were together,
Hal never really let go of his Navy days."

"Well, Mr. McGraw, I understand you have a
paper cut. Let's take a look."

With Skip adamant that they not find out the sex of their baby, Rita had secretly arranged for the sonogram technician to give her a coded signal.

The minimum age requirement for competitive youth sports continues it downward spiral.

"Man, *that* was low! Posing as the Publisher's Clearinghouse Prize Patrol to deliver a subpoena!"

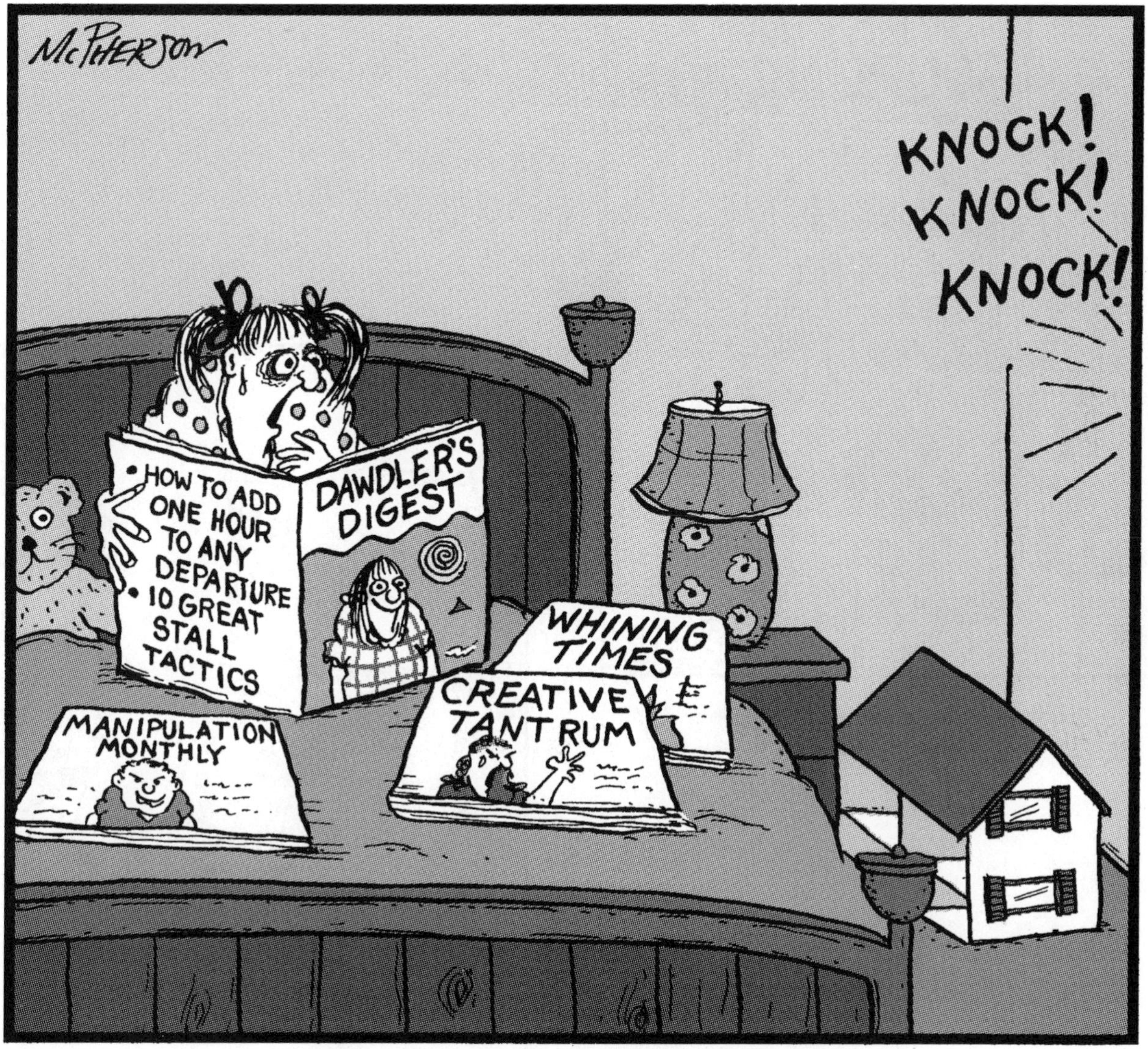

McPHERSON
KNOCK! KNOCK! KNOCK!
HOW TO ADD ONE HOUR TO ANY DEPARTURE
10 GREAT STALL TACTICS
DAWDLER'S DIGEST
WHINING TIMES
CREATIVE TANTRUM
MANIPULATION MONTHLY

"Ummm . . . just a minute, Mom!"

"Hey, do you want me to treat your psoriasis or not?"

Walt's battle to keep the squirrels out of the bird feeders takes a dark, new twist.

"Will you quit humming 'Bridge Over
Troubled Water'!"

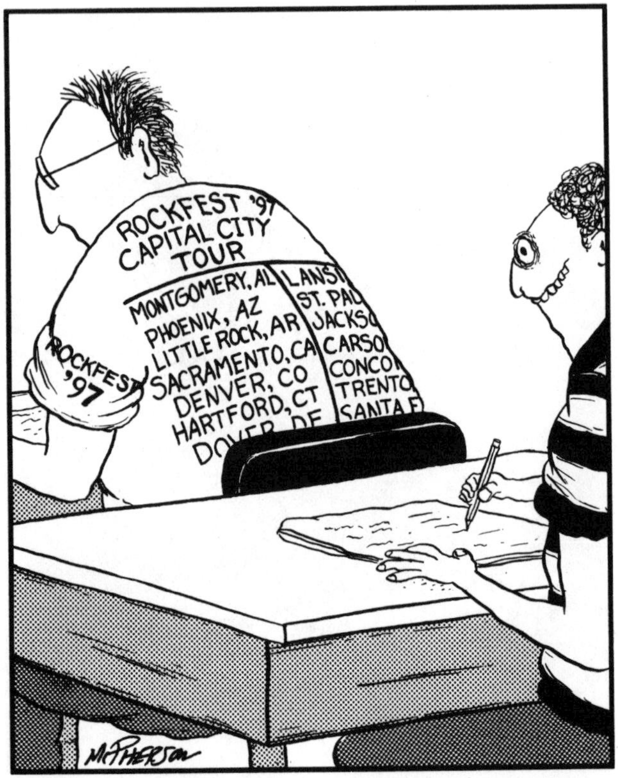
ROCKFEST '97
CAPITAL CITY
TOUR
MONTGOMERY, AL
PHOENIX, AZ
LITTLE ROCK, AR
SACRAMENTO, CA
DENVER, CO
HARTFORD, CT
ROCKFEST '97

Just when failing the geography midterm seemed certain, Mike made an astonishing discovery.

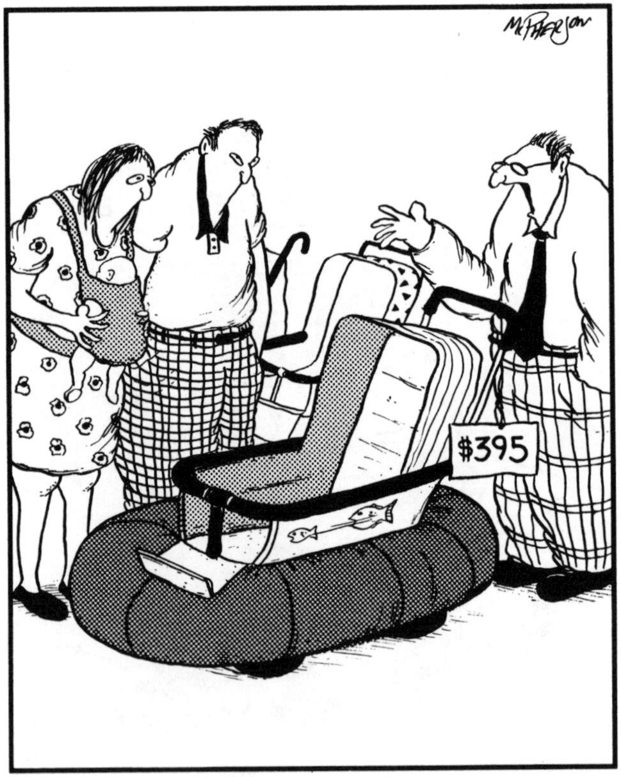
$395

"But hey, if you're not concerned about the threat of flash flooding and aren't 100 percent committed to your baby's safety, then maybe an amphibious stroller isn't for you."

"And how did you feel when the others in your foursome refused to give you that three-inch putt for eagle and you went ahead and missed it?"

"Don't snap at *me*! All I did was call their 800 number and say,
'Yes, I'd like to lose 10 pounds in 30 days guaranteed!'"

"I worked out a deal with the woman in the apartment next door. She handles all of Jason's diaper changes for a buck a pop."

"I'm sorry, sir. After further investigation, it turns out there was indeed a pinch of coconut in your dessert."

Warren callously devised a way to reserve himself a primo parking spot.

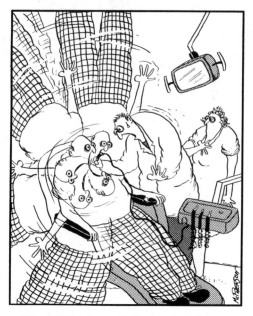

"The drill bit's jammed! Unplug the apparatus. UNPLUG IT!"

Microsoft and BarcaLounger™ team up to create
the world's first combination recliner-mouse.

"OK, hold on tight to those armrests, Mrs. Kilnhoff."

"It pays out in tokens good for one hour of free baby-sitting."

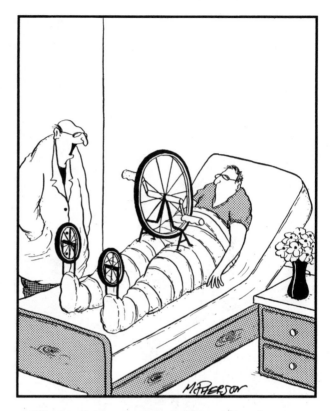

"Granted, the cast has to stay on for the next 37 weeks, but at least this way you can still get around."

To encourage fathers to take on more child-care responsibilities, Pampers comes out with its new line of sports-trivia diapers.

"If you think wearing that cheap cologne to bed is going to win points with me, you've got another thing coming!"

Management's latest attempt to keep employees from nodding off after lunch.

"Uh, folks, unfortunately I had this thing on pause the whole time. Would you mind re-enacting just the last 10 minutes?"

"Marge thinks I got it for quicker stock quotes, but I really bought it because my downloads from the Victoria's Secret Web site were taking forever."

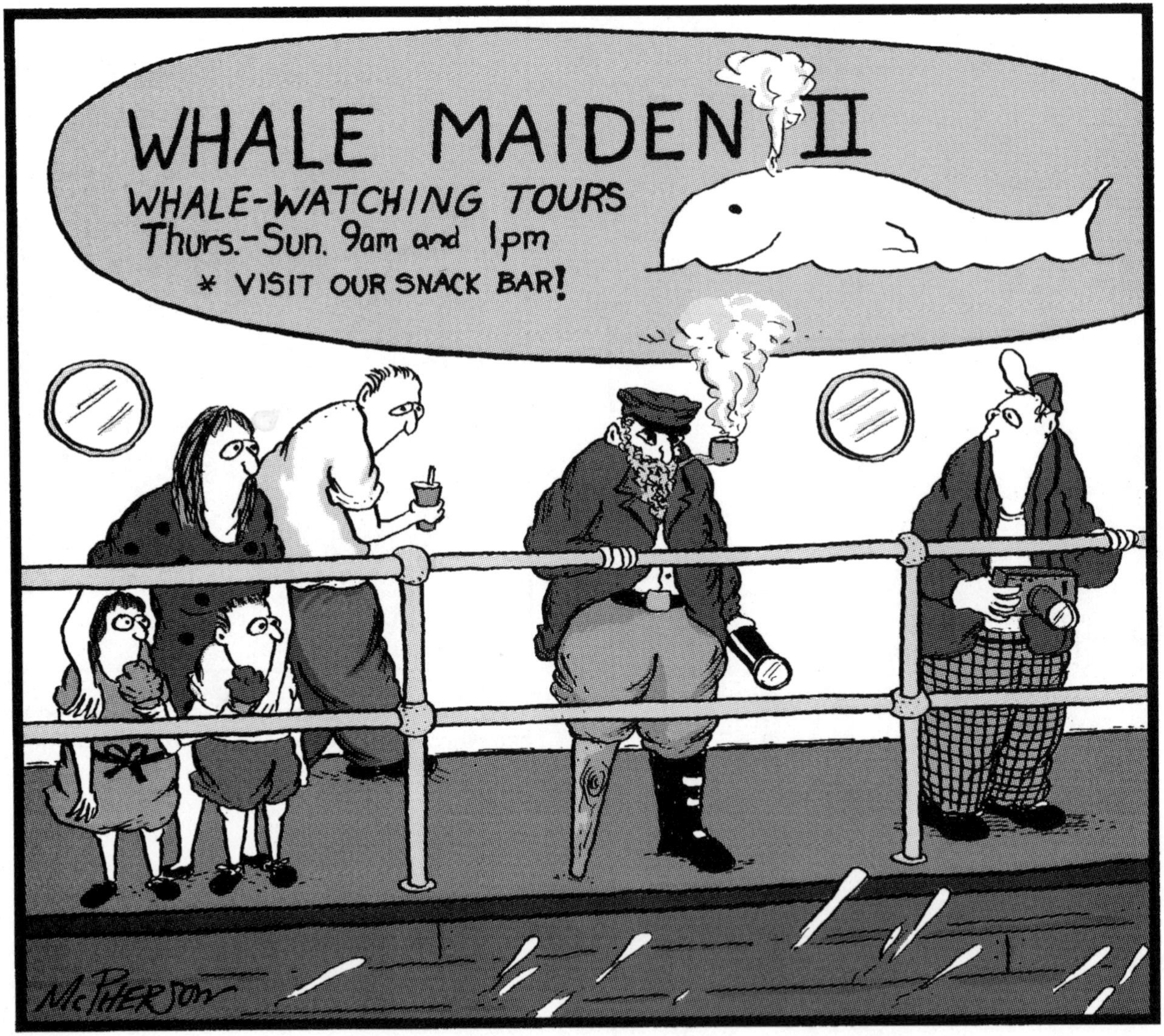
WHALE MAIDEN II
WHALE-WATCHING TOURS
Thurs.-Sun. 9am and 1pm
* VISIT OUR SNACK BAR!
McPHERSON

"Oh, that. The kids have started a shelter for neglected Giga Pets."

Carl's attempt to appear more intelligent than he really was backfired disastrously when his fake enlarged brain began to slip.

"You're going to play a song that *you* wrote about *me*?! I didn't even know you played an instrument! This is *so* romantic!"

Dr. Gremley reveled in this opportunity to turn the tables on his auto mechanic.

"And here, using enhanced sonogram technology, is a computer generated image of what your baby will look like when he's 50."

"Good news! We got rid of that rattle!"

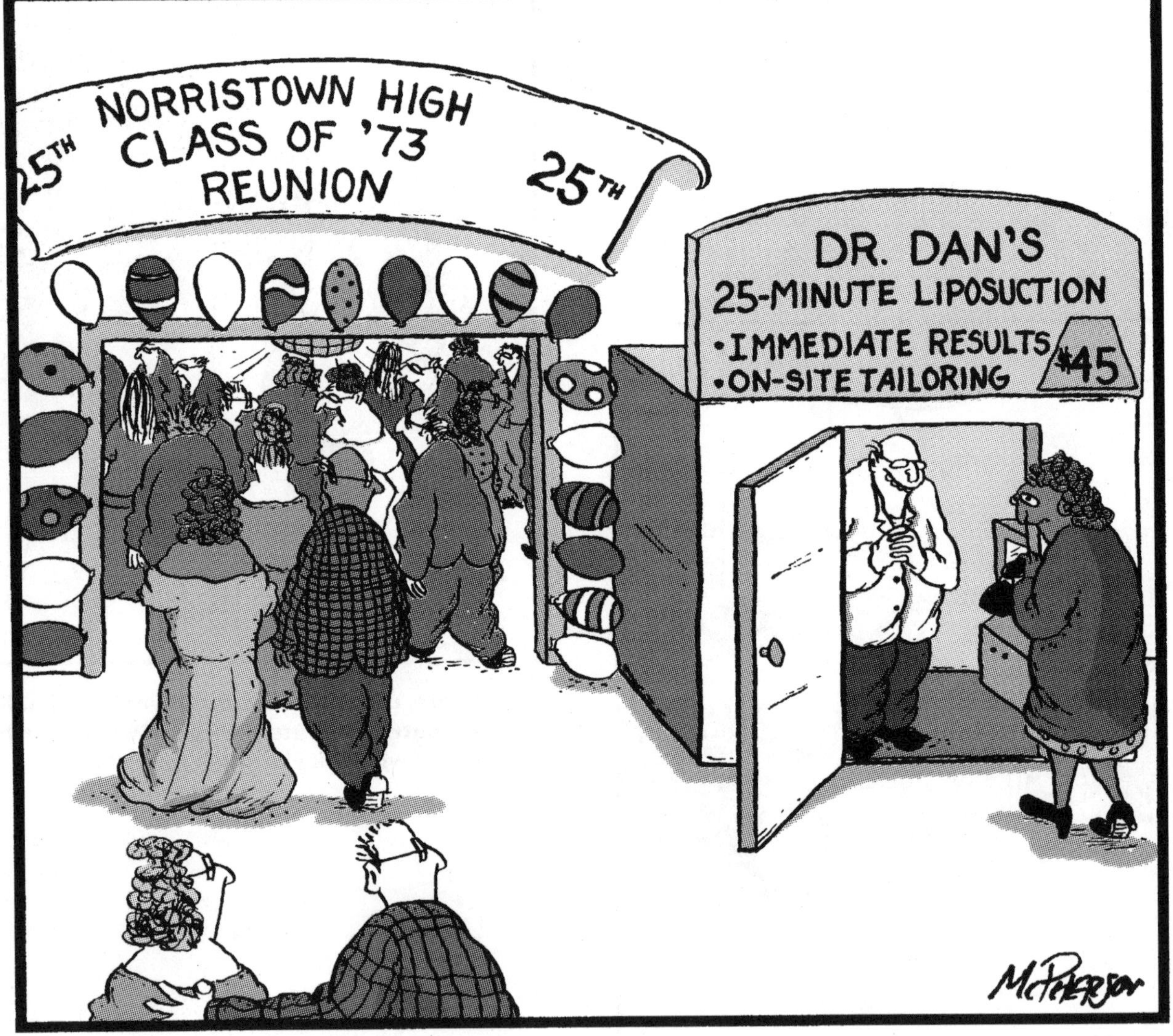
25TH
NORRISTOWN HIGH
CLASS OF '73
REUNION
25TH
DR. DAN'S
25-MINUTE LIPOSUCTION
•IMMEDIATE RESULTS
•ON-SITE TAILORING
$45
McPherson

"I should've known these bozos didn't have both oars in the water when they introduced themselves as Milton and Bradley."

To help better prepare its students for the real world, Ralston University simulates actual office conditions during final exams.

"I gotta find a new HMO."

"It's part of our new Campaign for
Increased Productivity."

"Oh, come on! Let's just take a little stroll on the beach. The fresh air will be good for you!"

"Oh, come on, Bruce! Where's your spirit of adventure?"

"Don't ask me how, but he fixed your leaky head gasket in 10 minutes.
Now he's taking care of that mysterious odor in the back seat."

Evel Knievel at age 86.

"Don't be alarmed, folks. The owners have agreed to replace the carpeting down here."

"Dave! These are all just part of the wallpaper pattern!"

57

With Ken off to the concession stand, Helen
donned her Spouse Finder Beacon™.

"If you spent any portion of our vacation fund on this thing,
I'm going to have to kill you."

"Best of all, it's 100 percent earthquake-proof."

To help relieve the boredom of their jobs, Joanne and Peggy installed a laugh track in the ladies' bathing suit department.

"No, it's not 2048; it's only two weeks later. Your check bounced."

Barbara's failure to make her high school cheerleading squad 25 years earlier was beginning to manifest itself in unhealthy ways.

"Come on! Where's your sense of humor? I'm not asking you to wear it for the entire operation, just until my husband conks out from the anesthesia!"

Ted learns an important lesson: *Never* let your
stomach growl when a member of your foursome
has a 3-foot putt for eagle.

By their third date, Ed began to sense that
Colleen just wanted to be friends.

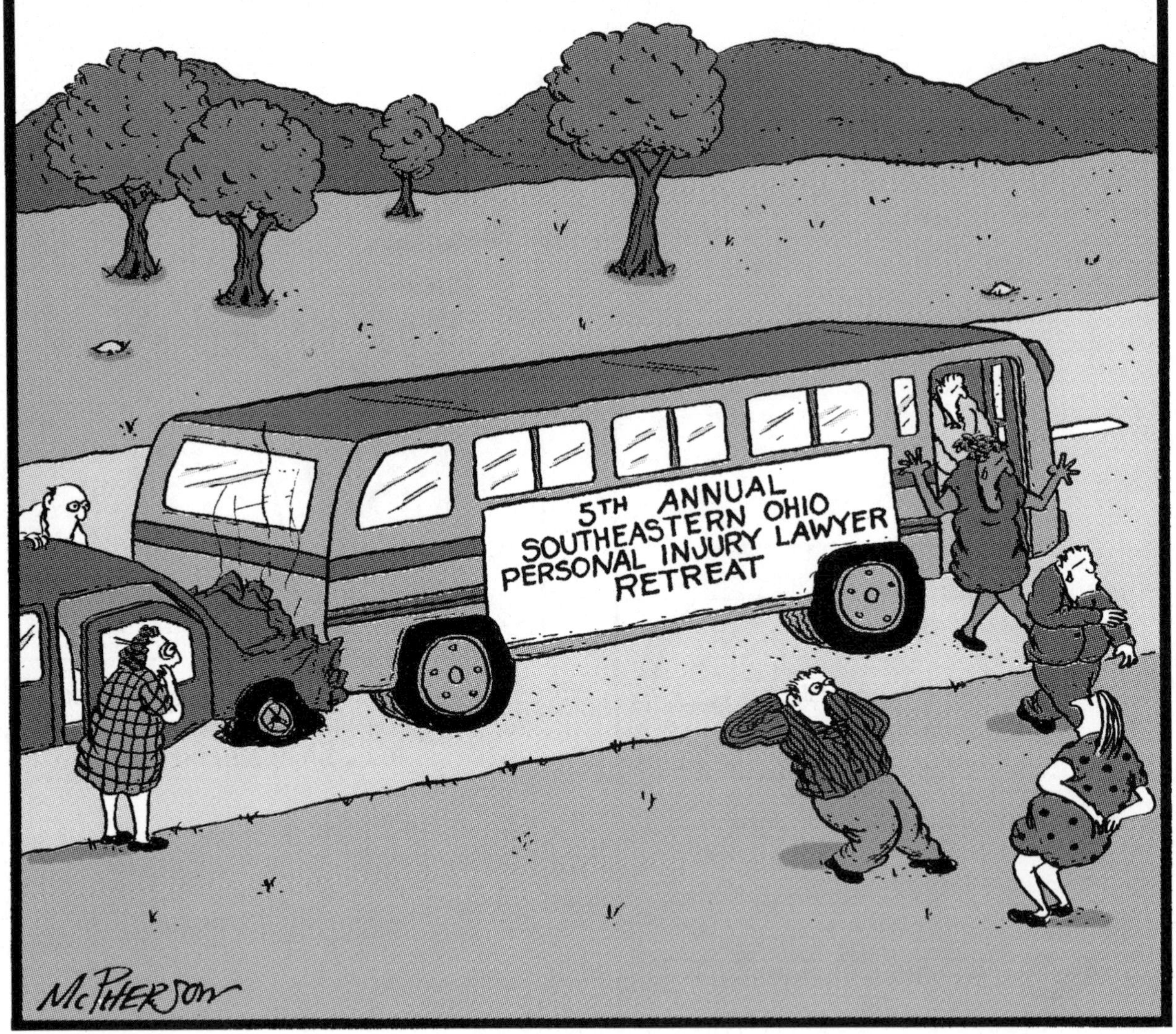
5TH ANNUAL
SOUTHEASTERN OHIO
PERSONAL INJURY LAWYER
RETREAT
McPHERSON

**Donations were up 42 percent since the church installed
a metal detector.**

"OK, *fine!* We'll flip for it! Heads, we do it *my* way; tails, we try Larry's stupid procedure!"

Carol Ann bravely volunteers to tackle the annual cleaning of the office microwave.

Realizing that a wipeout was inevitable, Raymond wisely hits the eject button on his in-line skates.

"OK, you say it's a tan '97 Lexus? . . . And what's the license plate number?"

As the band continued to play, an angry mob searched for members of the prom committee.

"Now, Gene, Dr. Radnor assured you that you wouldn't need stitches, and I'm sure he wouldn't lie."

"Could I interest you in our 'Catch Your Own Brook Trout' special for $13.95?"

Trycon Industries steps up its battle against inappropriate Net surfing by employees.

The face of golf is changed forever with the invention of mobile, dimple-sensing sand traps.

"The baby just said, 'Don't even *think* of naming me Trevor!'"

From the moment his mom announced that she had set up a family Web site, Gary knew he had entered a dark period in his life.

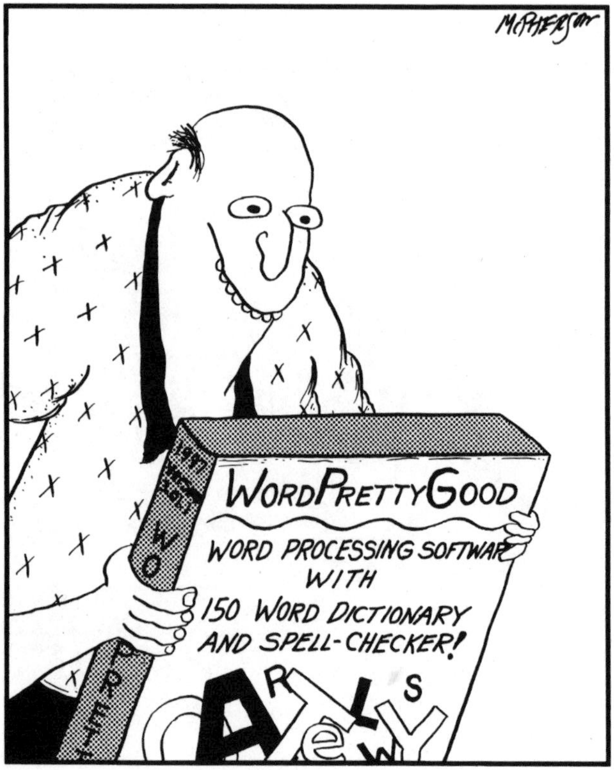
McPHERSON
WORDPRETTYGOOD
WORD PROCESSING SOFTWAR
WITH
150 WORD DICTIONARY
AND SPELL-CHECKER!

Budget software.

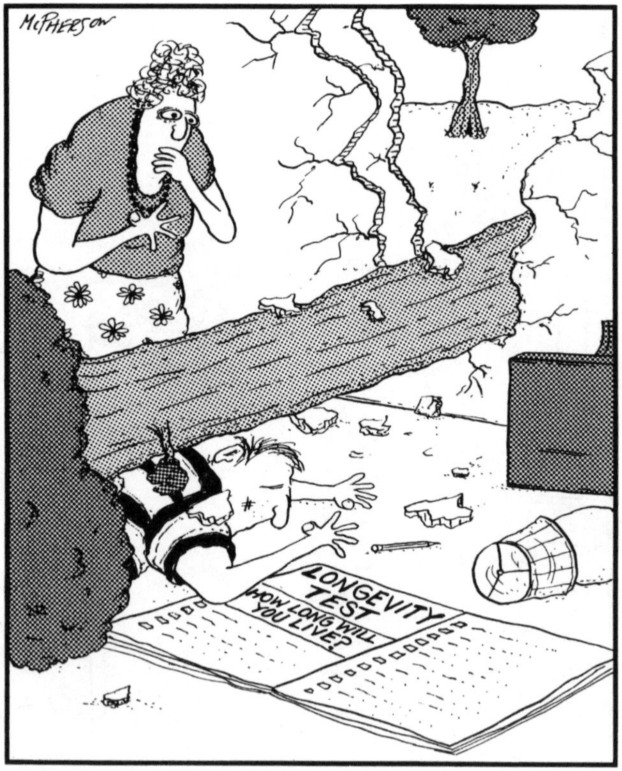
McPHERSON
LONGEVITY TEST
HOW LONG WILL YOU LIVE?

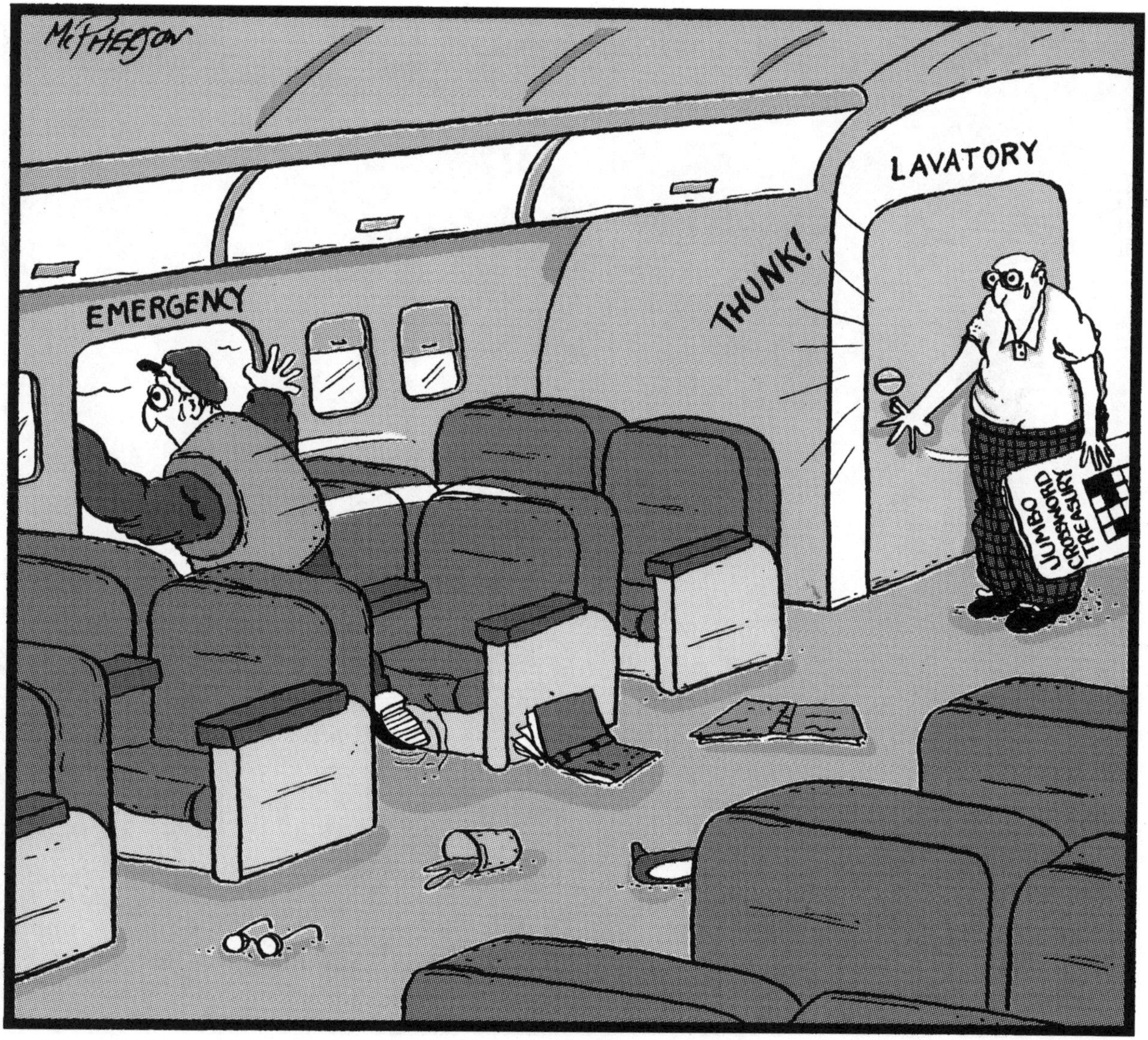
McPHERSON
LAVATORY
EMERGENCY
THUNK!
JUMBO CROSSWORD TREASURY

"Oh boy. That's a shame. I was *sure* I latched those doors properly. Oh well, looks as if the new house will be getting new furniture."

Deep into the Sunday Times crossword and hearing his boss approaching, Hal quickly rotated his Simulated Busy Desktop™ into place.

"Jerry, that's poison ivy you're rolling in."

"I'm sorry, folks, but the hospital is closed today in honor of the last episode of 'Seinfeld.'"

"Ooooh, look! *Nice* lawn mower! Lawn mower is our *friend*! Hey, there's Mr. Snow Shovel! *Good* Mr. Snow Shovel! Let's hang your new friend right above your crib!"

"Uh oh, Kelly! Look out! It's . . . EL NIÑO!"

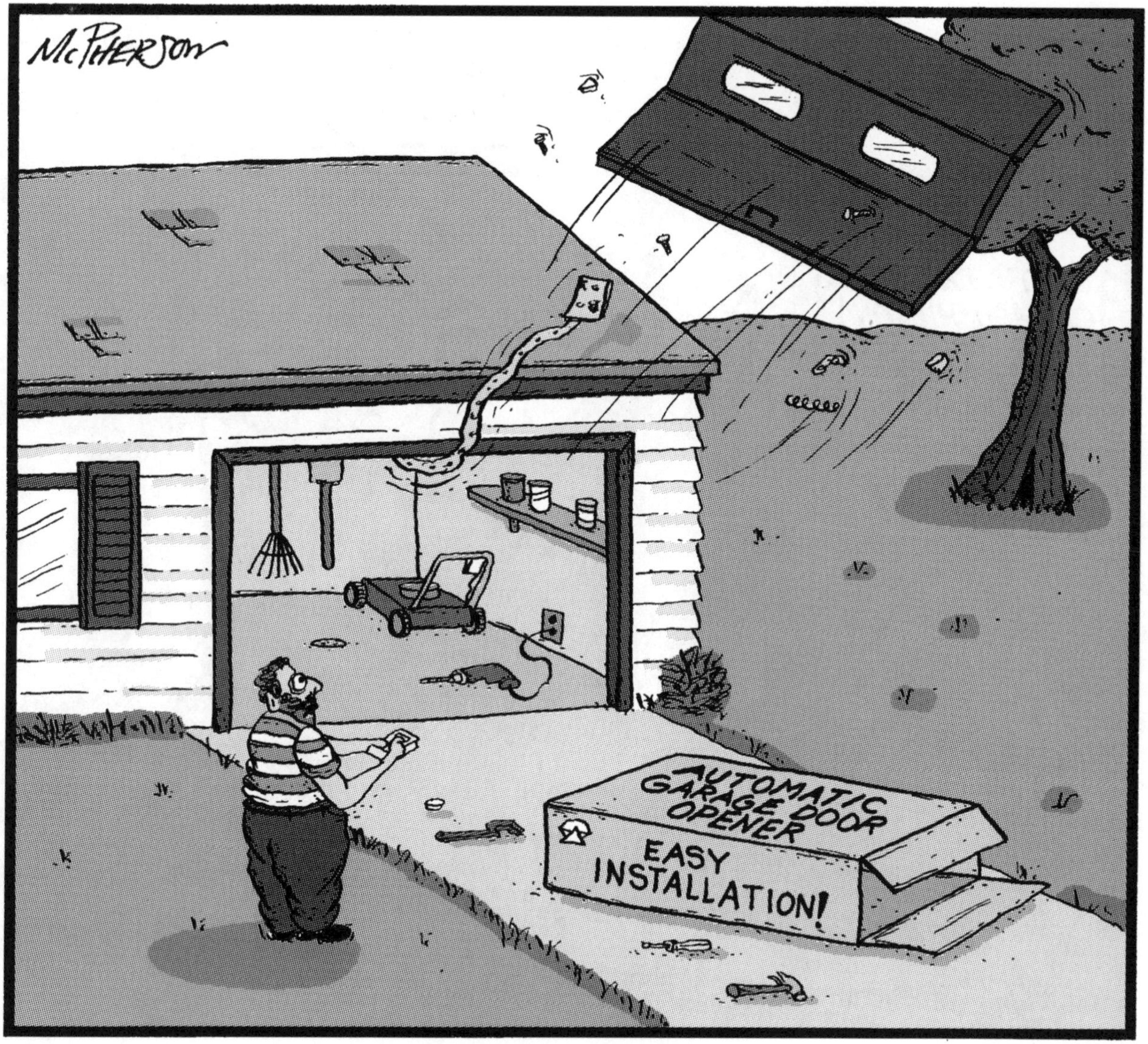
McPHERSON
AUTOMATIC GARAGE DOOR OPENER
EASY INSTALLATION!

Bob Villa at home.

When Muzak musicians go on tour.

THE 1998 MORTUARY EXPO!

GAP

WALDENBO

THE KING TUT

THE DAVEY JONES

THE SLIMLINE

THE ETERNITY

DOC FOSTER'S HOME EMBALMING KIT

Mall shows that bomb.

SAPPHIRE: MY COMPANY SPECIALIZES IN MAKING PLASTIC GNOMES.

DIRK: REALLY? MY COMPANY MAKES PLASTIC GNOMES TOO!

To her horror, Joyce suddenly realizes that the romantic stranger she's been cyber-chatting with for five months is Mr. Credley.

"Remember that recall notice you wadded up and
threw in the trash last week?"

"Polaroid No. 1: Ming's Chinese Laundry. Polaroid
2: 45 minutes later, same laundry. Oh, look!
What's that ahead? It's...Ming's Chinese Laundry!
Now do you believe we're driving in circles?!"

80

Hoping to make its graduation ceremony more entertaining, Cranston High enlisted the services of a fortune-teller.

"And now, in keeping with Dan's last request, I ask that each of you toss a handful of golf balls onto the casket while members of Sherwood Oaks Country Club give Dan a 21-titanium-driver salute."

Hoping to foster an environment of individuality and creativity, Zalco Industries encouraged employees to build their own cubicles.

"Sorry about this, Frank and Marge. It's just until
the kids get out of college."

"So then I said, 'A simple procedure that will give me better hearing than I've ever had, and without the hassle of a hearing aid?! Where do I sign?!'"

Another technological advancement for busy parents: the Clapper™-activated ejectable child's seat.

Having methodically acquired the names and addresses of the CEOs of every mail-order company that ever sent him an unsolicited catalog, Bert's five-year obsession comes to fruition.

"Since you can't eat solid foods for a week, we're pleased to offer you our new Virtual Reality Meal. Just chew on this rubber bulb, and you'll swear you're eating prime rib."

"Well, that's great that you don't have any pest problems, ma'am. Why don't you take our brochure anyway. Pests can strike at a moment's notice, you know."

"Hello?! Mr. Nemer? Is that you? Tap once if you're Mr. Nemer, twice if you're Mr. Sanchez! . . . Uh oh, Lois. We've got a *big* problem."

"Adding you to our car insurance as a teenager will triple our rate. From now on, wear this mask and overcoat, and go by the name 'Uncle Mort.'"

Finding Bob sound asleep and knowing that his big presentation to the board was in 10 minutes, his co-workers pulled the old camp prank of placing his hand in a glass of warm water.

To keep passengers' heads upright while they slept, Mercury Airlines introduced their new helium-filled Slumber Bonnets™.

Tired of being chastised by their 3-year-old for not knowing all the "Thomas the Tank Engine" characters, the Gertmans wisely invested in flash cards.

"It's the last diaper-wipes container we ever used. We had it mounted after the twins were potty trained."

Russ foolishly ordered the Sense-a-tron option when he signed up for the Weather Channel.

90

Having spotted their angry wives, the foursome quickly sought
the safety of the course's Emergency Spouse Shelter.

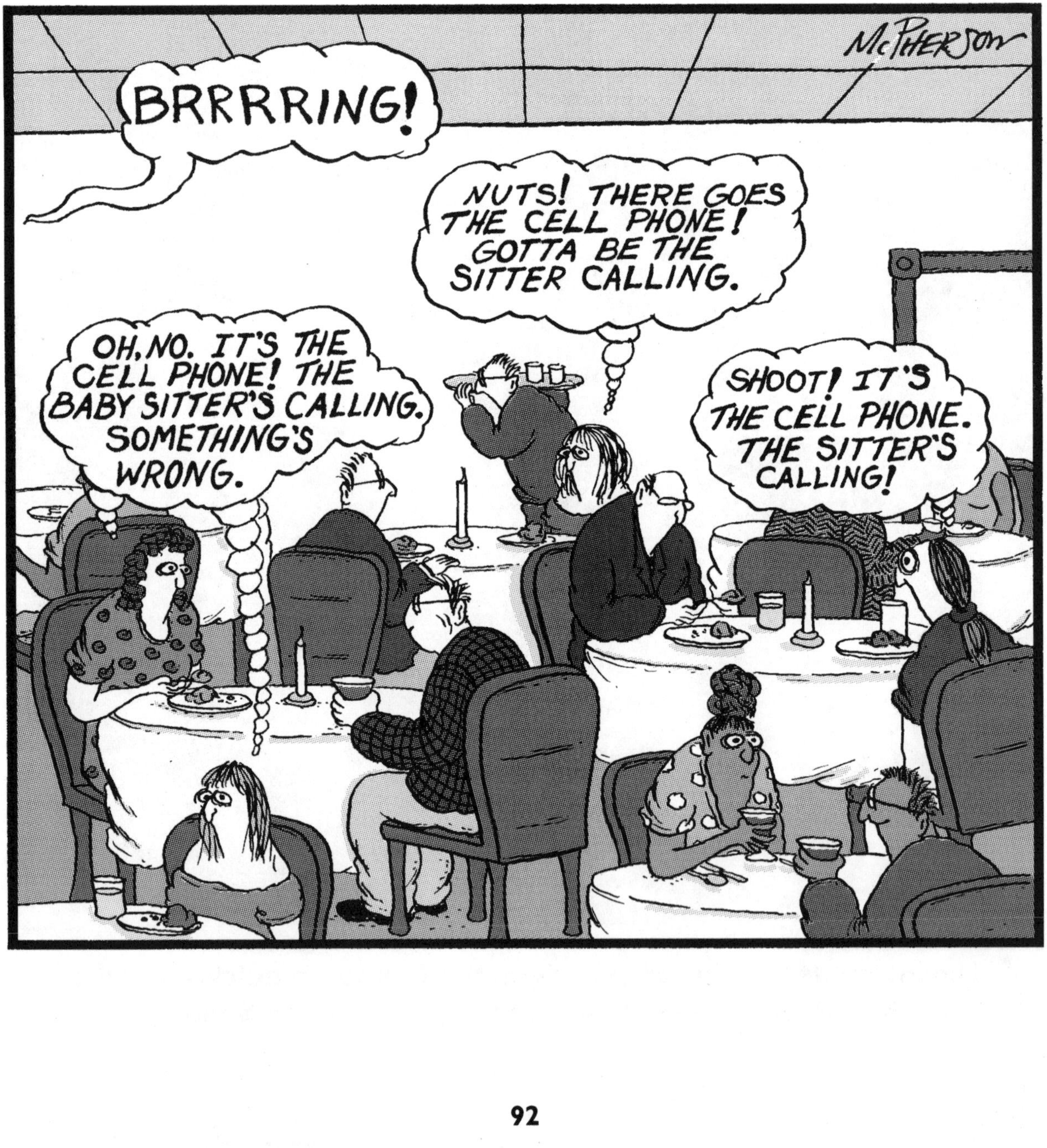
McPHERSON
BRRRRING!
NUTS! THERE GOES THE CELL PHONE! GOTTA BE THE SITTER CALLING.
OH, NO. IT'S THE CELL PHONE! THE BABY SITTER'S CALLING. SOMETHING'S WRONG.
SHOOT! IT'S THE CELL PHONE. THE SITTER'S CALLING!

The four basic types of co-workers.

"Are you insane?! When I said I smelled an odor, I meant you should change his diaper, not slap one of those deodorizing discs on him!"

When nurses party.

"Hey, Dad! Guess what! A man came up to Mom
on the beach and asked her if she'd like to
audition to be the 1999 Thigh master
Before-and-After Woman!"

"Fire one more warning round over their heads
and if they still don't let us play through,
take out their cart."

The nation's health care system continues to become more and more specialized.

To help employees feel more in touch with their children, the company day-care center incorporated a creative new design concept.

Even at this early stage, the Gurnleys sensed a
subtle competition between the
Hortons' baby and theirs.

Bill's co-workers slowly began to suspect that he had lied about having a master's degree in computer science.

"What do you *mean* you forgot to buy film?!"

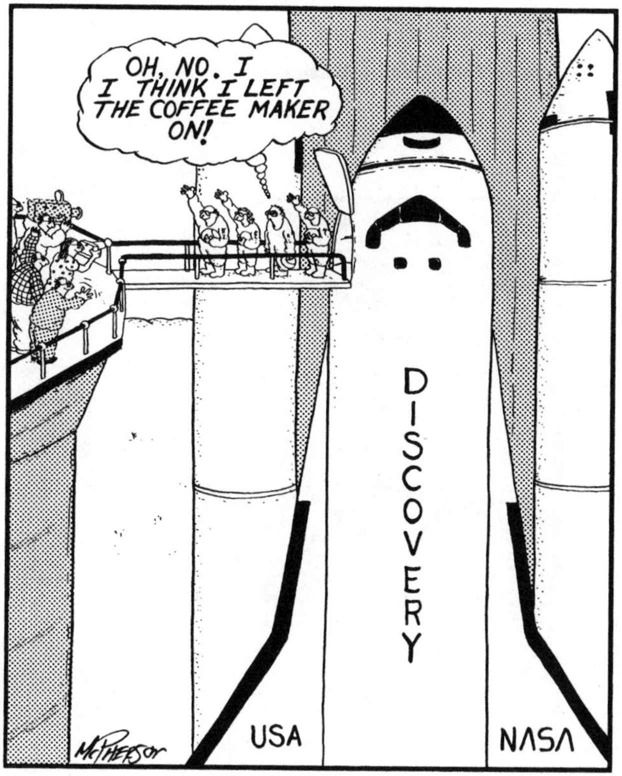
OH, NO. I
I THINK I LEFT
THE COFFEE MAKER
ON!
DISCOVERY
USA
NASA
McPHERSON

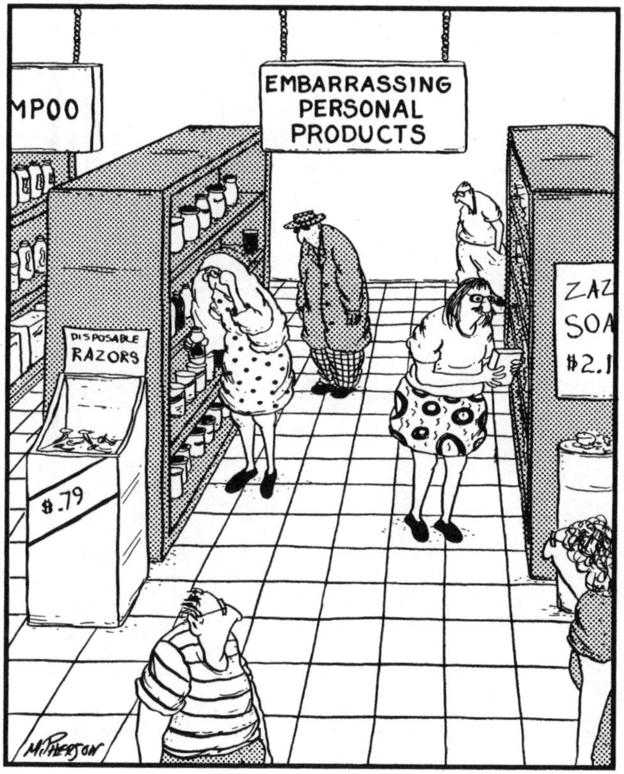
EMBARRASSING
PERSONAL
PRODUCTS
MPOO
DISPOSABLE
RAZORS
$.79
ZAZ
SOA
$2.1
McPHERSON

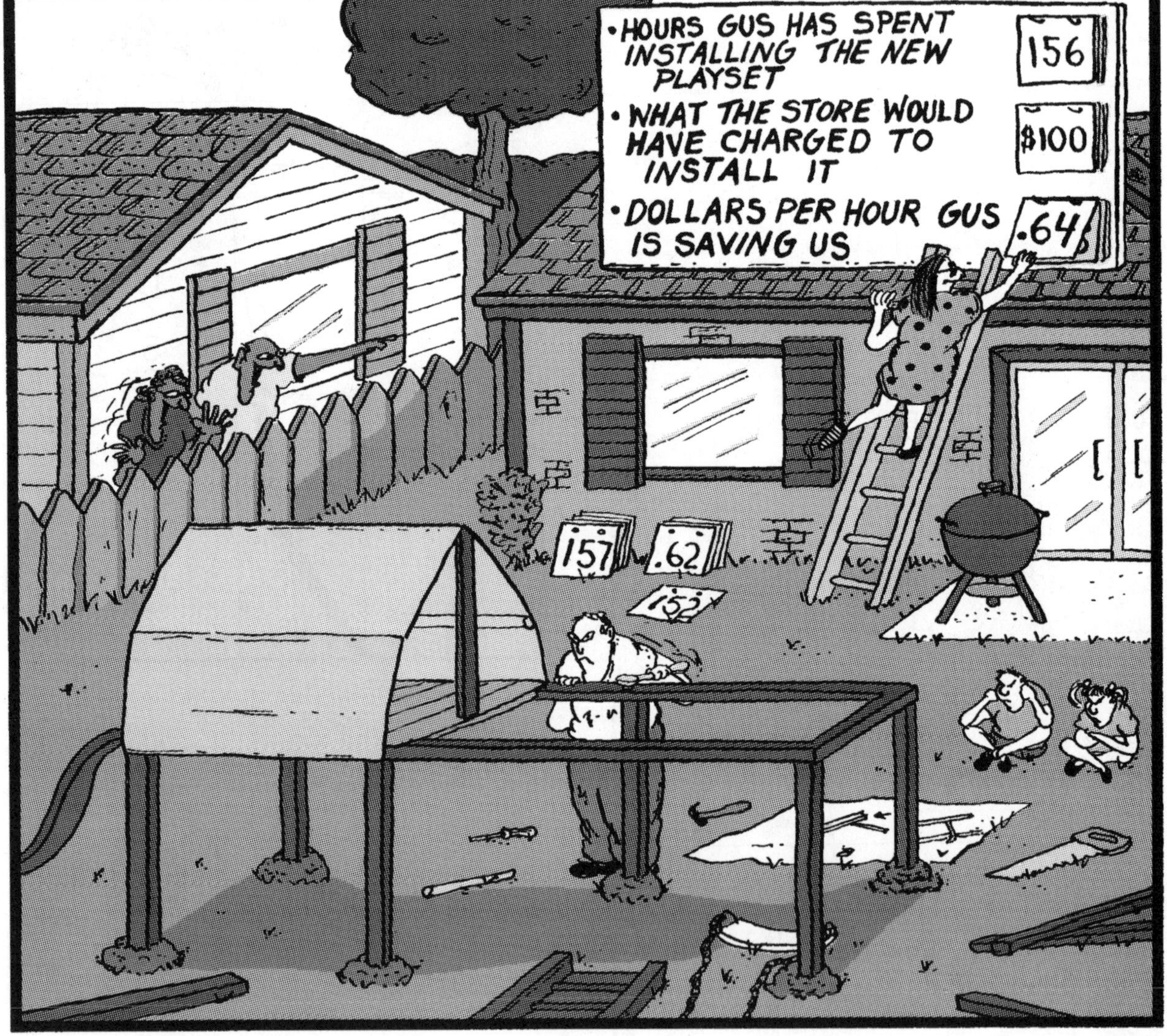

•HOURS GUS HAS SPENT INSTALLING THE NEW PLAYSET
156
•WHAT THE STORE WOULD HAVE CHARGED TO INSTALL IT
$100
•DOLLARS PER HOUR GUS IS SAVING US
.64
157
.62
152

Another sign that the honeymoon is over.

The boys down at Witt Construction were having hours of fun with their new **Nerf** wrecking ball.

It was not until their wedding night that Jason was able to grasp the full scope of Amanda's online addiction.

"Kevin, if you don't say the blessing, you're going to make God very, very angry."

Before taking kids to the Burger Baron, Linda wisely installed her new fast-food tarp.

By shrewdly disguising its employees as fortune-tellers, Northmont Air was able to lure customers away from other airlines.

"Sir, we are not discriminating against people with birthmarks. We just feel that it's best for everyone if you stay out of the water right now."

An angry public strikes back at the Eighth Annual National Telemarketers Banquet.

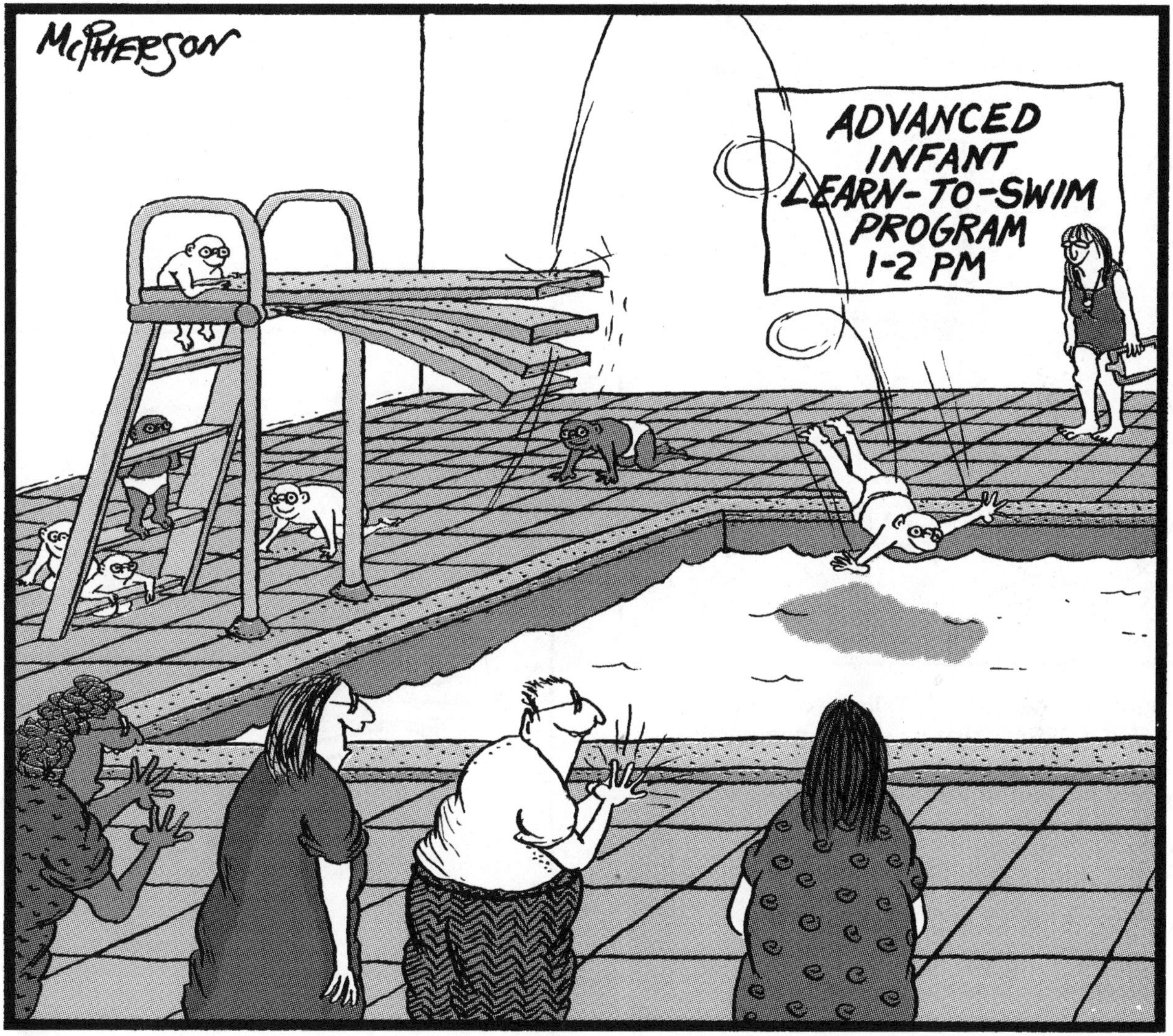
McPHERSON
ADVANCED INFANT LEARN-TO-SWIM PROGRAM 1-2 PM

Summer employees at Yellowstone make the amazing discovery that by simultaneously flushing all 66 toilets in their dormitory, they can get Old Faithful to erupt anytime they want.

"Well, maybe now you'll know better than to raise
your hand the next time they ask for a volunteer
from the audience."

"He was 29, living in L.A. I came across this
big musty box of baseball cards just cluttering up
the house, so I tossed them. Today, they'd be
worth $80,000."

The Dortford County Sheriff's Department introduces its new electromagnetic speed-enforcement system.

"Anchors? What do you mean, 'anchors'? Those are umbrellas, silly!"

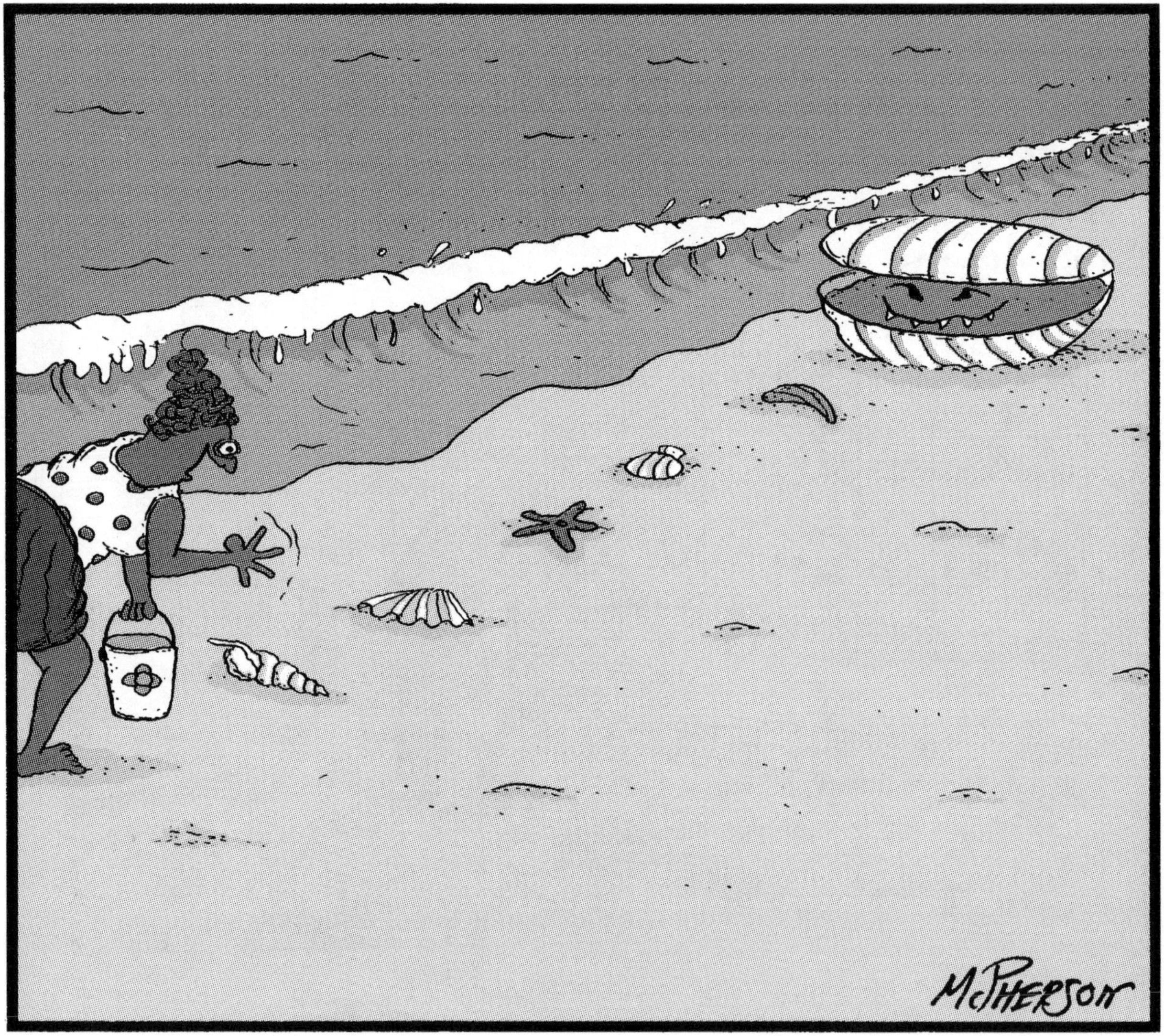
McPHERSON

"Your fettuccine calamari is going to be another 10 or 15 minutes."

At Jerry Springer's family reunion.

"Joe! It's the landlord!"

"No. 2, step forward and take three full swings."

"And here's a feature I *know* you're going to love!
It's got a built-in audio sensor that sends a mild
electric jolt to the back seat anytime it detects
the phrase, 'Are we there yet?'"

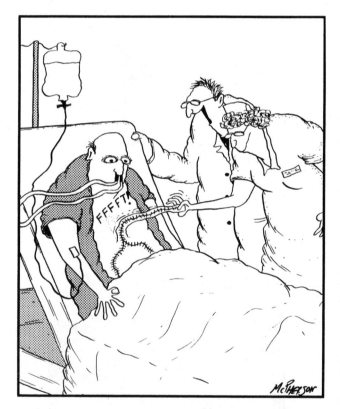

"Now that you're fully recovered, Mr. Dawkins, we
can tell you the truth. The 12-hour operation, the
intravenous meals, the three weeks of bed rest ...
all were part of an elaborate placebo effect."

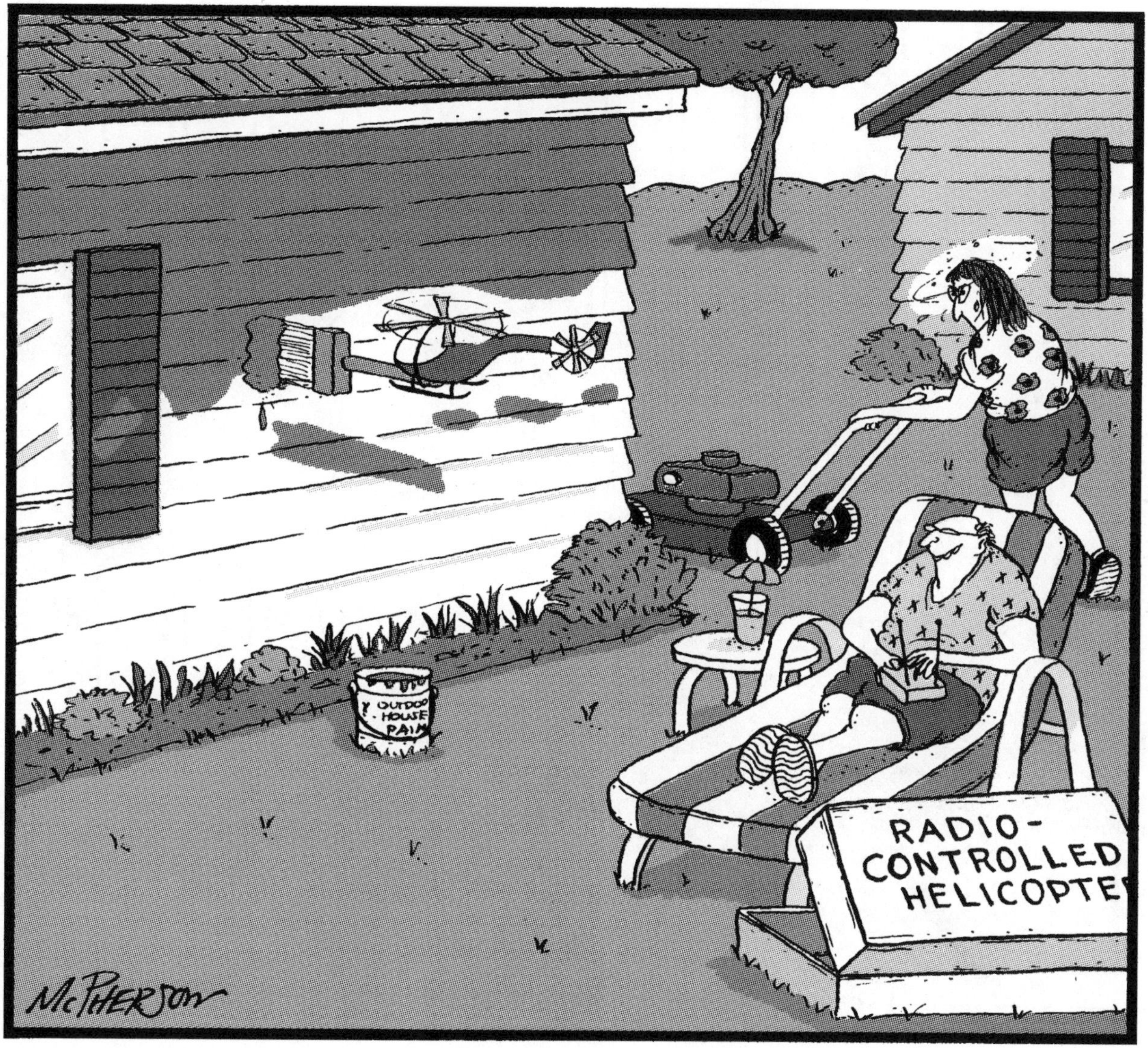
OUTDOOR HOUSE PAIN
RADIO-
CONTROLLED
HELICOPTE
McPHERSON

"It's a rejection letter from that masonry job you applied for!"

"Hey, Marie. You didn't happen to see a . . . oh, there it is."

Blatco Industries makes a desperate attempt to get employees to read the company newsletter.

It was bad enough when Bill headed into the bath-
room carrying the Sunday paper. Now a new evil
was entering Gracie's life.

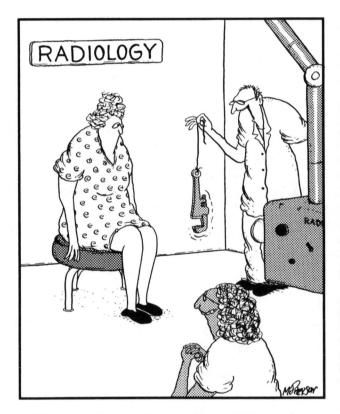

"Hey. Mrs. Dubner, help us play a little prank on
Dr. Goodman. Just clench this thread between
your teeth so the pipe wrench is dangling in front
of your stomach while we take some X-rays."

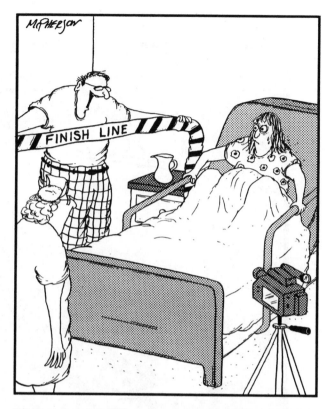

"Oh, come on! Where's your sense of humor? Just let me tape it to your knees and get some video footage while the midwife is delivering the baby."

A disturbing new development in the art world: ballet hecklers.

Hoping to add even more excitement to its races, NASCAR introduces the Egg-in-a-Spoon Relay 500.

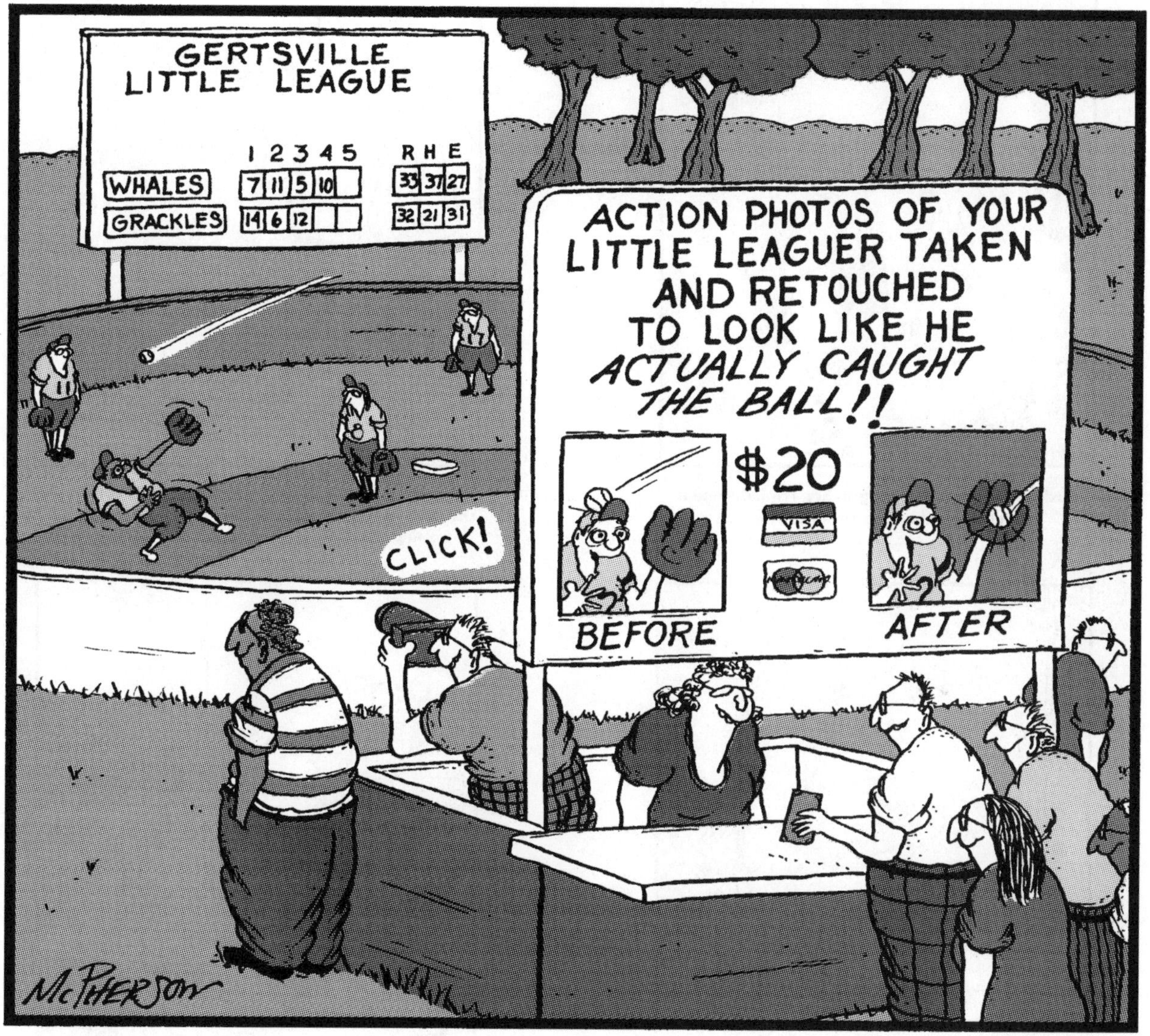
GERTSVILLE LITTLE LEAGUE
1 2 3 4 5 R H E
WHALES 7 11 5 10 33 37 27
GRACKLES 14 6 12 32 21 31
ACTION PHOTOS OF YOUR LITTLE LEAGUER TAKEN AND RETOUCHED TO LOOK LIKE HE ACTUALLY CAUGHT THE BALL!!
$20
VISA
BEFORE
AFTER
CLICK!
McPHERSON

Business at Zeke's Driving Range tripled since it added the exploding ceramic statues.

"Nearly all of our diagnoses are done by computer these days. Please open your mouth and say 'Aaah' while pressing your face into the scanner."

"So now, when you want to make the bed, you just give this rope one good yank and—voilà!"

Overwhelmed by the rigors of raising a 3-year-old and 10-month-old twins, Kim unilaterally opts for zone coverage.

"Weird! First there's a hornet's nest attached to your golf bag, and now there's one on your lounge chair! Maybe it's an omen that today's *finally* the day to start painting the house!"

"I'm sorry, dear, but I've been asking you to slow down for the last three hours and you just ignored me. So at the last rest stop, I went to a pay phone and reported you."

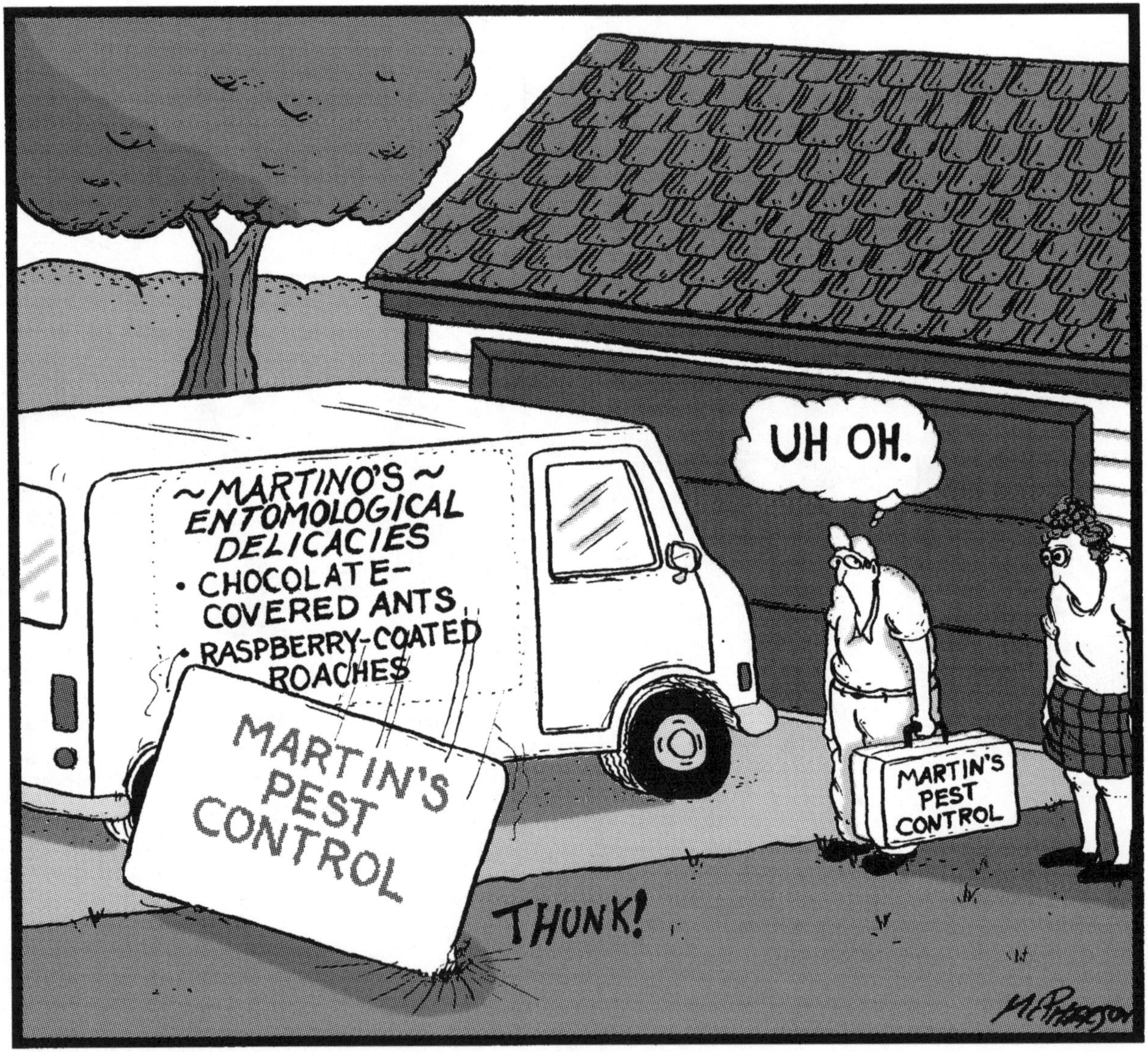
~MARTINO'S~
ENTOMOLOGICAL
DELICACIES
• CHOCOLATE-
COVERED ANTS
• RASPBERRY-COATED
ROACHES
MARTIN'S
PEST
CONTROL
UH OH.
MARTIN'S
PEST
CONTROL
THUNK!

"What? Oh, them. They're here from that TV show 'Medical Bloopers and Blunders' just in case something interesting happens."

"Go take off his oxygen mask for a second and ask him if he knows anything about fuel pumps."

To ensure that their kids get out the door on time each day, the Waxleys shrewdly installed a hydraulically operated living room floor.

Researchers study Toddler Long Distance Syndrome: the phenomenon whereby 2-year-olds playing with telephones invariably make 98 percent of their calls to the five most expensive places on earth.

"Are you kidding?! Twenty-five bucks is a steal! It's only been used twice!"

In a technological breakthrough that would stun the world, a leading auto manufacturer develops a car that runs on kids' meal toys.

"The magazine says, 'Improve Your Hearing Without Hearing Aids or Surgery! Immediate Results! Only $50!' Yep, you got ripped off, all right."

Striving to avoid controversial line calls, the professional tennis tour adopts a jury system.

Saving herself hours of cleanup time, Carol wisely outfitted Justin with a personal toy rake.

"He must have thought that mole on your back was a fly."

"I thought for sure we had that train beat."

"Isn't that neat?! We had the baby's heartbeat recorded on CD!"

Once a year, thousands gather in Carlisle, Pa., to witness the pageantry, grace, and beauty of the National Synchronized Lawn-Mowing Championships.

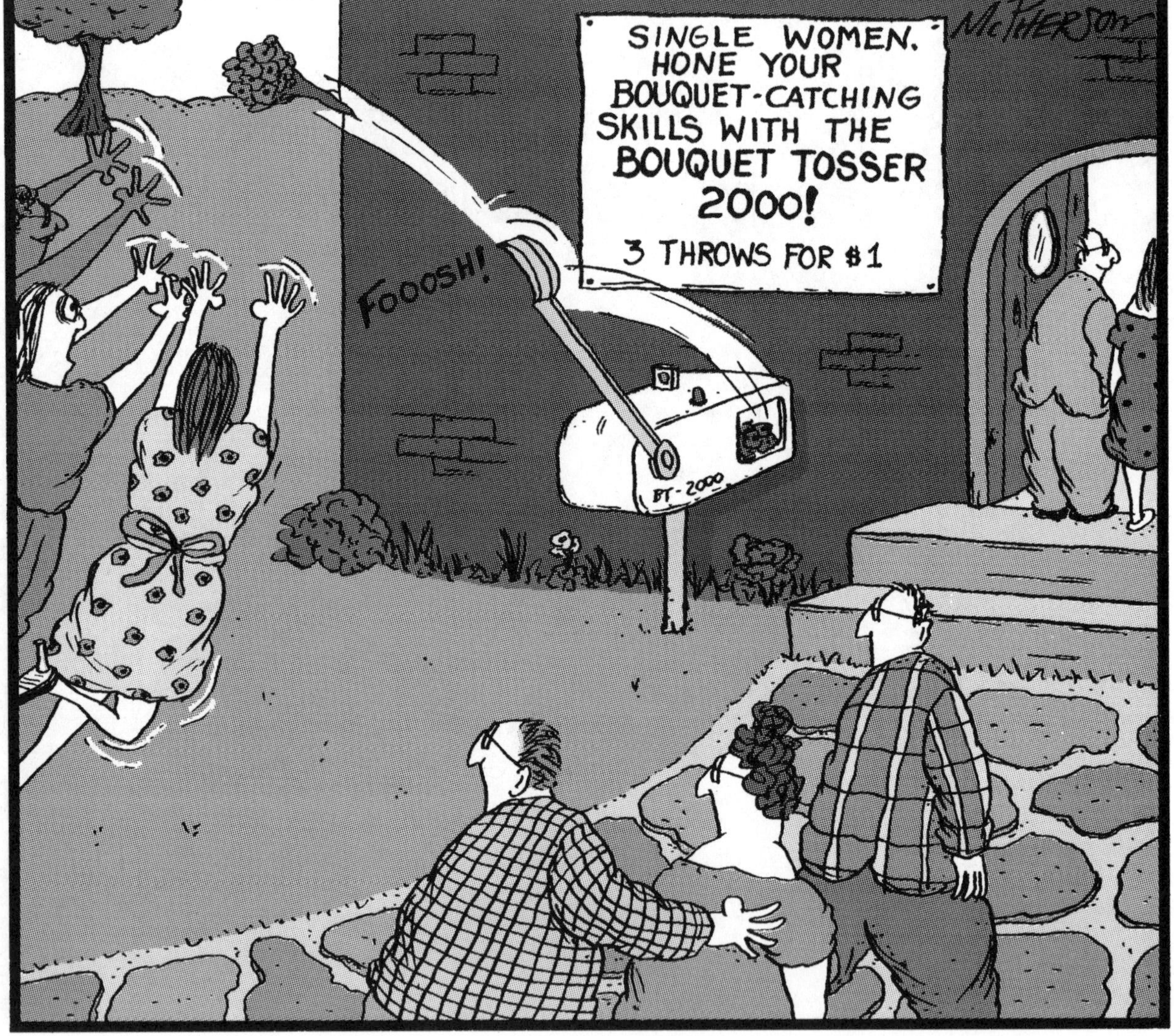
SINGLE WOMEN.
HONE YOUR
BOUQUET-CATCHING
SKILLS WITH THE
BOUQUET TOSSER
2000!
3 THROWS FOR $1
FOOOSH!
BT-2000

"I came in here to fix the leaky faucet, noticed the toilet paper holder was loose, and one thing sort of led to another. What time is everyone coming for the dinner party?"

"Phillip, tell the nice people you are sorry, *now*!"

"The cell-phone company said that to expand their coverage, they needed to build a tower five feet northwest of our couch. They gave me $500 and, get this, Hon, a *free cell phone!*"

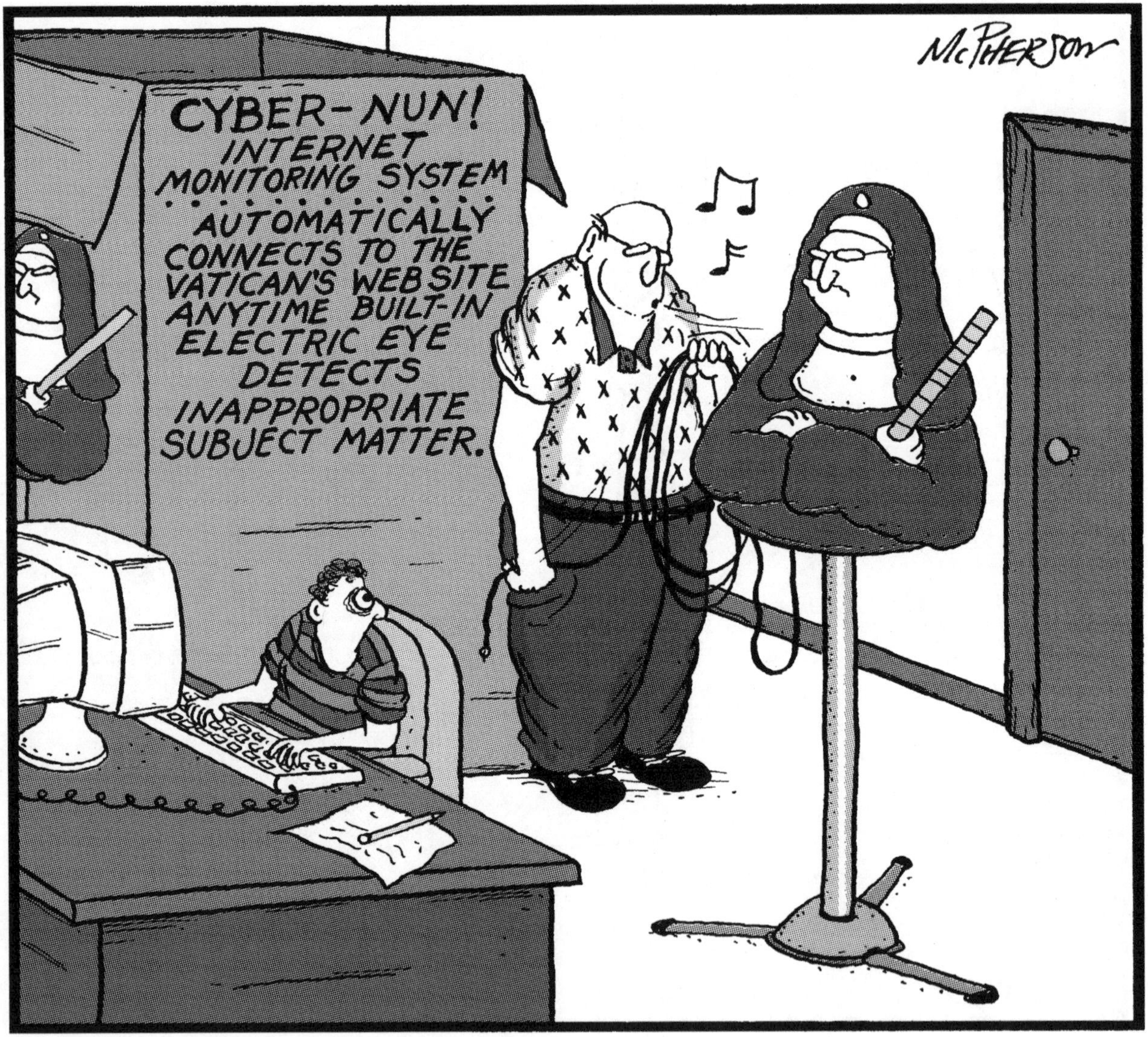
McPHERSON
CYBER-NUN!
INTERNET
MONITORING SYSTEM
AUTOMATICALLY
CONNECTS TO THE
VATICAN'S WEBSITE
ANYTIME BUILT-IN
ELECTRIC EYE
DETECTS
INAPPROPRIATE
SUBJECT MATTER.

"You've got two options. We can treat you right here and now, or you can wait until five more people come in with broken arms and get our group discount."

Designs for golf's new oversized drivers have begun to spiral out of control.

"We don't like to use chemicals on the animals. I'm going to use this trumpet to scare the fleas toward Scamp's tail, where they'll jump off into that pan of scalding hot water."

"I'm sure you're right ma'am! The treadmill's computer must have been wrong. You probably burned way more than 113 calories!"

"You missed a section here. We need to have the serial number and tensile strength of each of the seat belts in your car before we can process your registration."

139

"There you go again! You're snapping at me, Alan!"

"Calm down, Mr. Dortford! We just want to take a gag photo
for the hospital newsletter!"

Movie theater thermostats.

"Tired of jerks who refuse to dim their high beams? When you buy this car, it's payback time!"

To help break up the routine, many farmers have instated formal Fridays.

"OK, Tommy! Fun time's over! Push the button to lower the window! Tommy! Push the button!"

142

"Well, there's your problem! You need to rotate your image 90 degrees counterclockwise, plus your trimming level is set way too low."

"Yeah, right! That makes sense! Let's go spend $150 for a new VCR just because the rewind mechanism on this one is broken, when our power drill rewinds tapes just fine!"

143